ALL TIME FAVORITE COUNTRY SONGS FOR EASY PIANO

ISBN 0-634-01569-9

HAL•LEONARD®
CORPORATION

7777 W. BLUEMOUND RD. P.O. BOX 13819 MILWAUKEE, WI 53213

AIN'T GOIN' DOWN
('Til the Sun Comes Up)

Words and Music by KIM WILLIAMS,
GARTH BROOKS and KENT BLAZY

Bright Country

Six o'-clock on Fri-day eve-ning, Ma-ma does-n't know she's leav-ing
Nine o'-clock, the show is end-ing but the fun is just be-gin-ning.

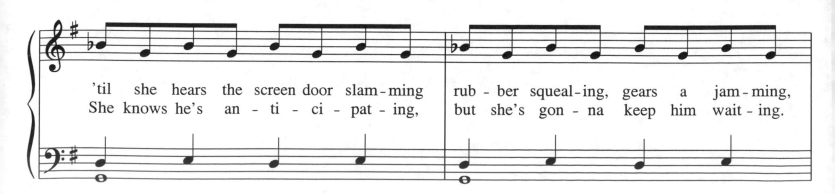

'til she hears the screen door slam-ming rub-ber squeal-ing, gears a jam-ming,
She knows he's an-ti-ci-pat-ing, but she's gon-na keep him wait-ing.

C

lo - cal Coun - try sta - tion just a | blar - ing on the ra - di - o.
First, a bite to eat and then they're | head - ing to the hon - ky- tonk, but

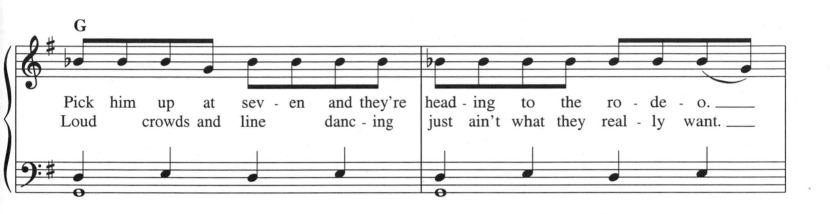

G

Pick him up at sev - en and they're | head - ing to the ro - de - o. ____
Loud crowds and line danc - ing | just ain't what they real - ly want. ____

D

Ma - ma's on the front porch, | scream-ing out a warn - ing: "Girl, you'd
Drive out to the boon - docks | and park down by the creek, where it's

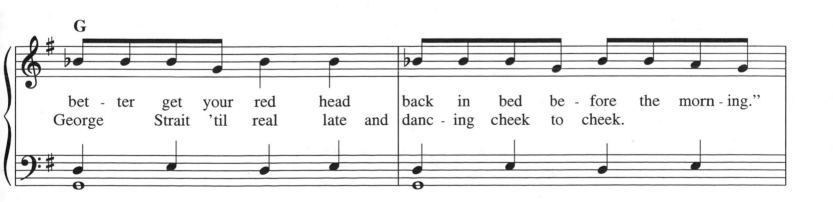

G

bet - ter get your red head | back in bed be - fore the morn - ing."
George Strait 'til real late and | danc - ing cheek to cheek.

4

They ain't go - ing down 'til the

sun comes _ up, ain't giv-ing in 'til they get e-nough.

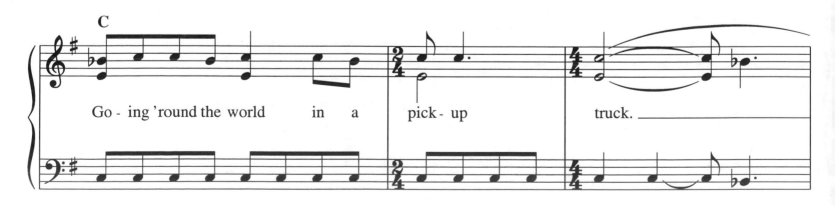

Go- ing 'round the world in a pick - up truck. _____

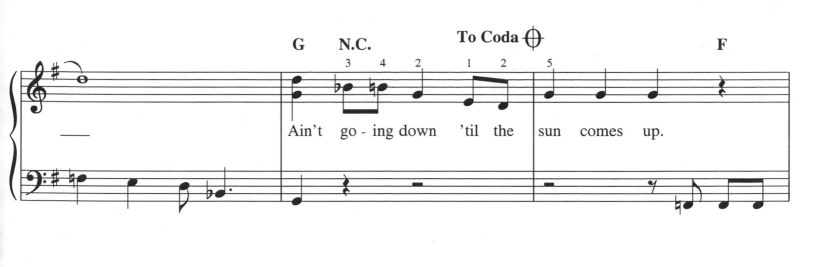

Ain't go - ing down 'til the sun comes up.

Ten 'til twelve is wine and danc - ing. Mid - night starts the hard ro - man - cing.
Six o' - clock on Sat - ur - day, her Folks don't know he's on his way. The

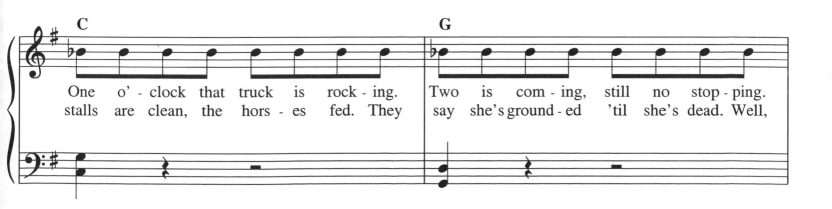

One o' - clock that truck is rock - ing. Two is com - ing, still no stop - ping.
stalls are clean, the hors - es fed. They say she's ground - ed 'til she's dead. Well,

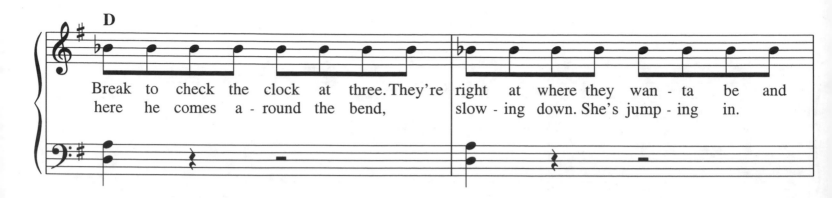

D

Break to check the clock at three. They're right at where they wan-ta be and
here he comes a-round the bend, slow-ing down. She's jump-ing in.

G

four o'-clock get up and go-ing. Five o'-clock that roost-er's crow-ing.
Hey, Mom, your daugh-ter's gone and There they go a-gain. Hey.___

1.

Hey. Yeah, they

2.

D.S. al Coda

They

CODA

sun comes up. Yeah.

BLUE EYES CRYING IN THE RAIN

Words and Music by
FRED ROSE

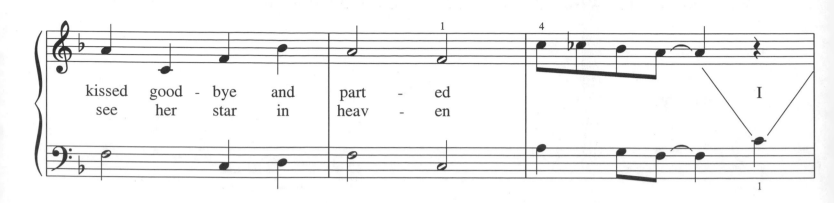

kissed good - bye and part - ed
see her star in heav - en

I

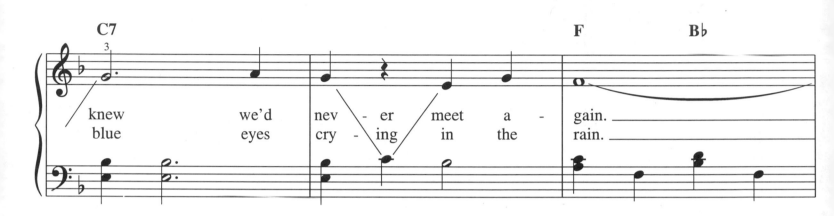

C7

knew we'd nev - er meet a - gain.
blue eyes cry - ing in the rain.

F **B♭**

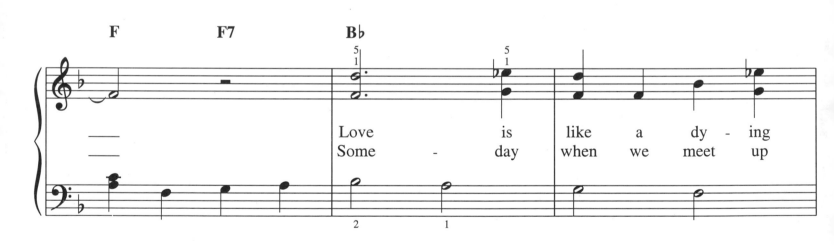

F **F7** **B♭**

Love is like a dy - ing
Some - day when we meet up

em - ber
yon - der

F

on - ly
we'll stroll

mem - o - ries re - main. _____
hand in hand a - gain. _____

Through the ag - es I'll re - mem - ber
In a land that knows no part - ing

blue eyes cry - ing in the
blue eyes cry - ing in the

1.
rain. _____

2.
rain. _____

BIG BAD JOHN

Words and Music by
JIMMY DEAN

Moderately

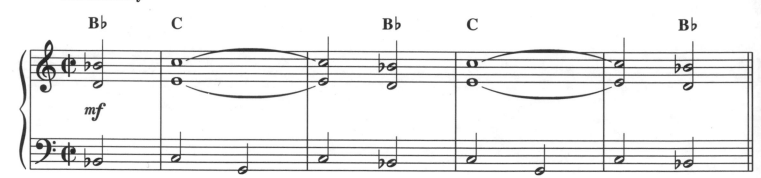

Verse: *Vamp (background for recitation)*

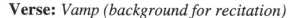
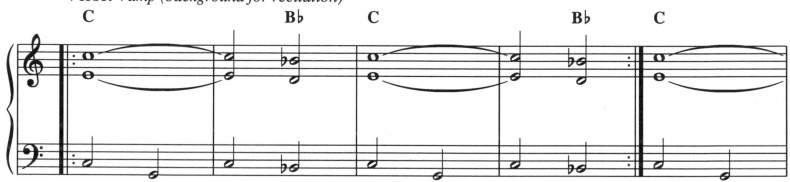

Refrain *(after each recitation)*

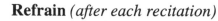
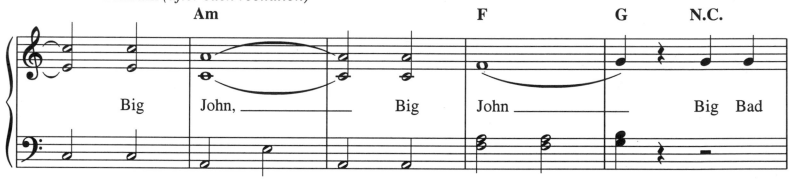

Big   John, _____   Big   John _____   Big   Bad

To Verse

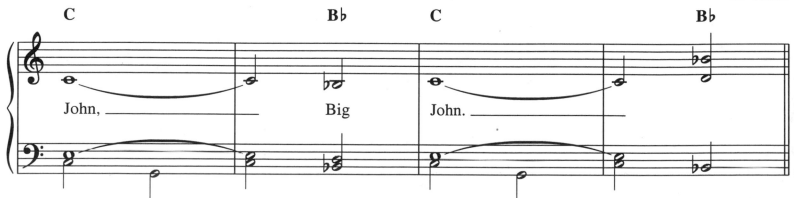

John, _____   Big   John. _____

Recitation

Verse 1:   Every morning at the mine you could see him arrive,
He stood six-foot-six and weighed two-forty-five.
Kind of broad at the shoulder and narrow at the hip,
And everybody knew you didn't give no lip to Big John!
(Refrain)

Verse 2:   Nobody seemed to know where John called home,
He just drifted into town and stayed all alone.
He didn't say much, a-kinda quiet and shy,
And if you spoke at all, you just said, "Hi" to Big John!
Somebody said he came from New Orleans,
Where he got in a fight over a Cajun queen.
And a crashing blow from a huge right hand
Send a Louisiana fellow to the promised land. Big John!
(Refrain)

Verse 3:   Then came the day at the bottom of the mine
When a timber cracked and the men started crying.
Miners were praying and hearts beat fast,
And everybody thought that they'd breathed their last 'cept John.
Through the dust and the smoke of this man-made hell
Walked a giant of a man that the miners knew well.
Grabbed a sagging timber and gave out with a groan,
And, like a giant oak tree, just stood there alone. Big John!
(Refrain)

Verse 4:   And with all of his strength, he gave a mighty shove;
Then a miner yelled out, "There's a light up above!"
And twenty men scrambled from a would-be grave,
And now there's only one left down there to save; Big John!
With jacks and timbers they started back down
Then came that rumble way down in the ground,
And smoke and gas belched out of that mine,
Everybody knew it was the end of the line for Big John!
(Refrain)

Verse 5:   Now they never re-opened that worthless pit,
They just placed a marble stand in front of it;
These few words are written on that stand:
"At the bottom of this mine lies a big, big man; Big John!"
(Refrain)

BOOT SCOOTIN' BOOGIE

Words and Music by
RONNIE DUNN

15

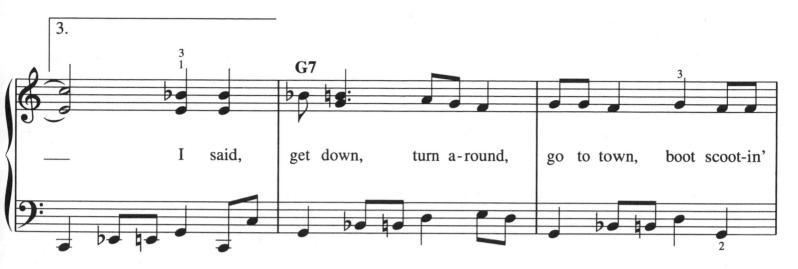

Additional Lyrics

4. The bartender asks me, says,
   "Son, what will it be?"
   I want a shot at that red head younder lookin' at me.
   The dance floor's hoppin'
   And it's hotter than the Fourth of July.
   I see outlaws, inlaws, crooks and straights
   All out makin' it shake doin' the boot scootin' boogie.

CRAZY

Words and Music by
WILLIE NELSON

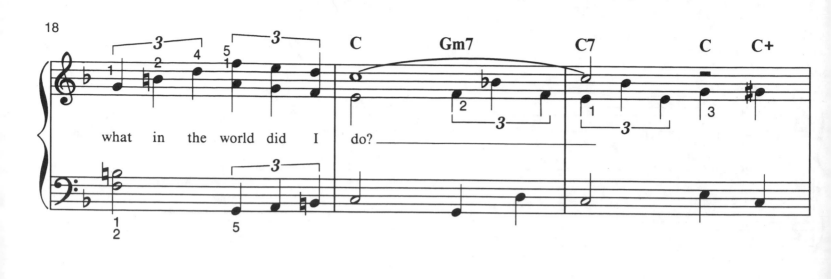

what in the world did I do? _____

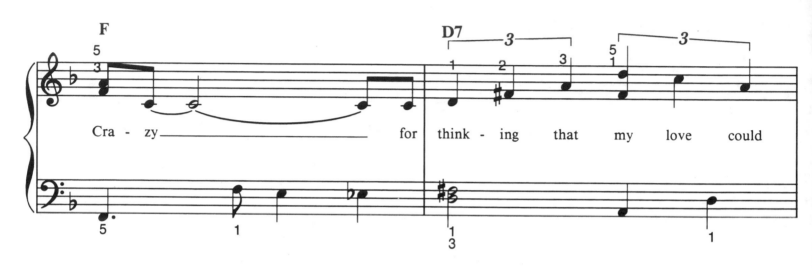

Cra - zy _____ for think - ing that my love could

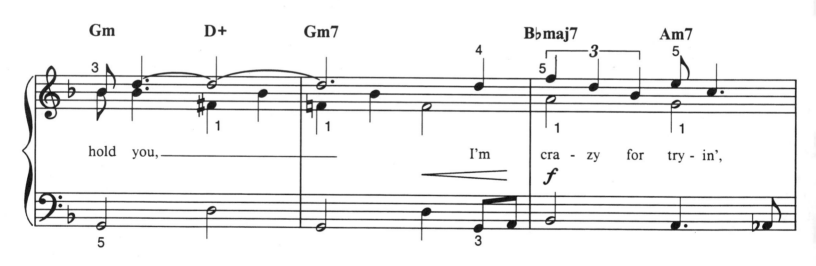

hold you, _____ I'm cra - zy for try - in',

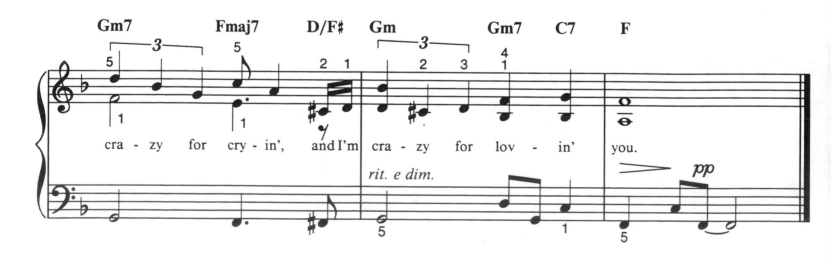

cra - zy for cry - in', and I'm cra - zy for lov - in' you.

rit. e dim.

ELVIRA

Words and Music by
DALLAS FRAZIER

Moderately

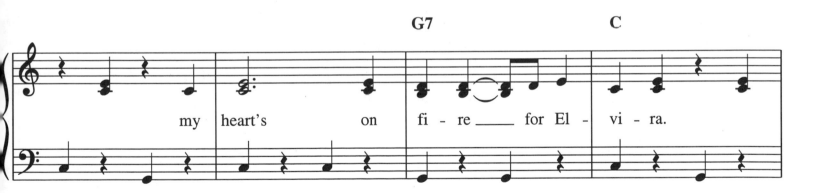

El - vi - ra, El -vi - ra,

my heart's on fi - re ____ for El - vi - ra.

Eyes that look like heav - en, lips like cher - ry
night I'm gon - na meet her at the Hun - gry House Ca -

G7

wine,   that girl can sho' nuff make my lit - tle light shine. _____
fe.   And I'm gon-na give her all the love _ I can. _____

C   F7

_____   I get a fun - ny feel - ing   up and down my
            She's gon-na jump and hol - ler   'cause I saved up my last two

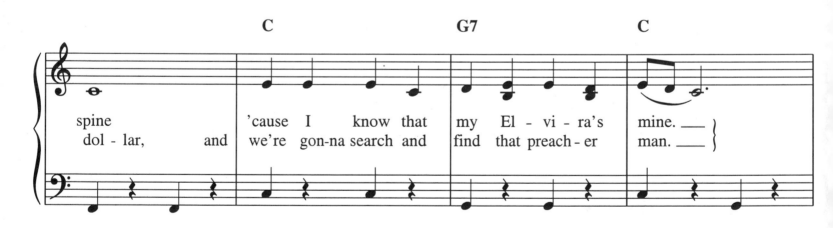

C   G7   C

spine   'cause I   know that my El - vi - ra's mine. ___ }
dol - lar,   and we're gon-na search and find that preach - er man. ___ }

I'm sing-in' El - vi - ra,   El - vi - ra,

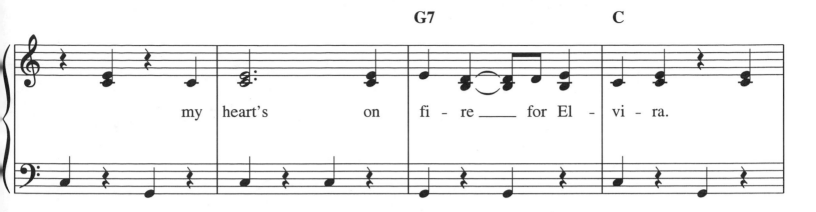

my heart's on fi - re ____ for El - vi - ra.

Gid -dy - up, a oom pa - pa oom pa - pa mow mow,

gid-dy-up, a oom pa-pa oom pa-pa mow mow, hi - yo Sil - ver a -

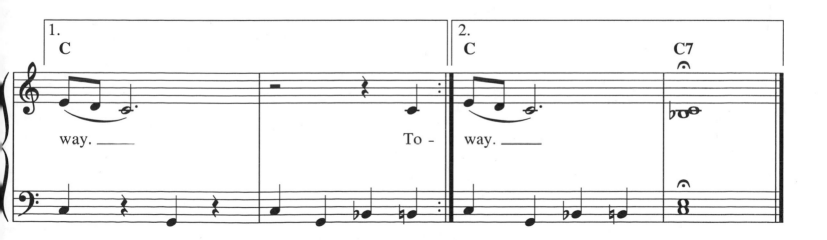

way. ____   To -   way. ____

DADDY'S HANDS

Words and Music by
HOLLY DUNN

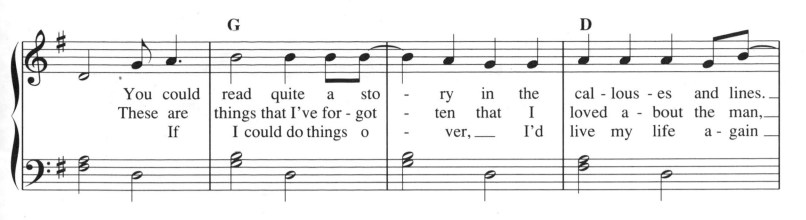

You could read quite a sto - ry in the cal - lous - es and lines.
These are things that I've for - got - ten that I loved a - bout the man,
If I could do things o - ver, __ I'd live my life a - gain

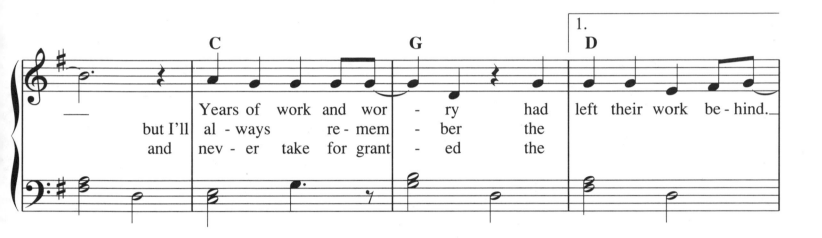

Years of work and wor - ry had left their work be - hind.
but I'll al - ways re - mem - ber the
and nev - er take for grant - ed the

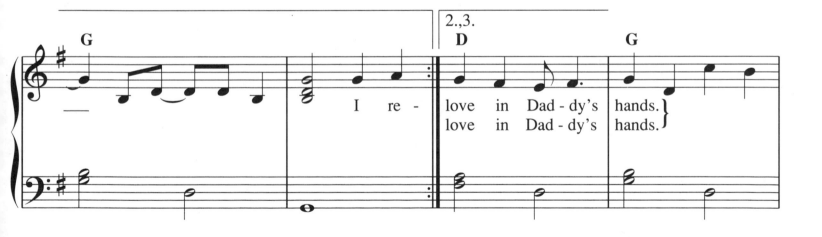

I re - love in Dad - dy's hands.
love in Dad - dy's hands.

Dad - dy's hands __ were soft and kind when I was cry -

24

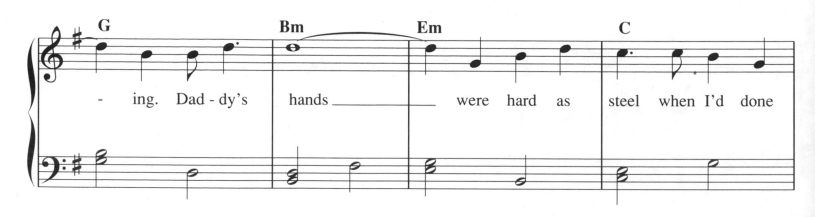

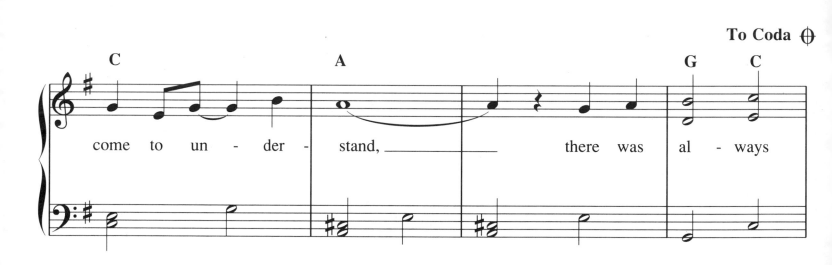

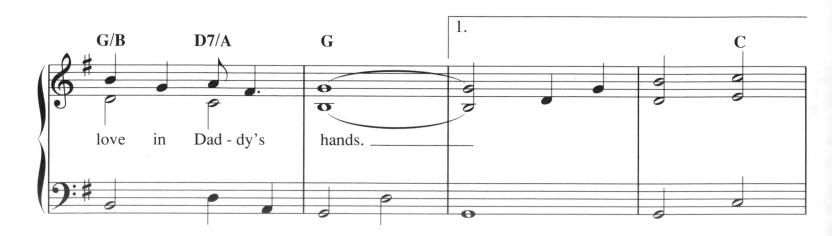

FOR THE GOOD TIMES

Words and Music by
KRIS KRISTOFFERSON

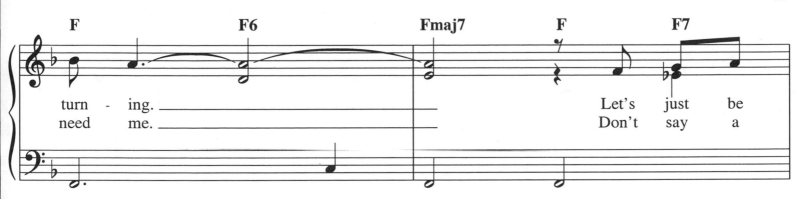

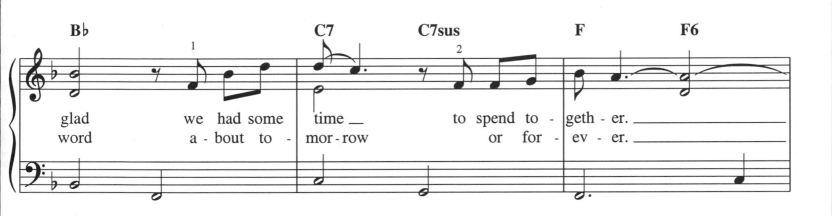

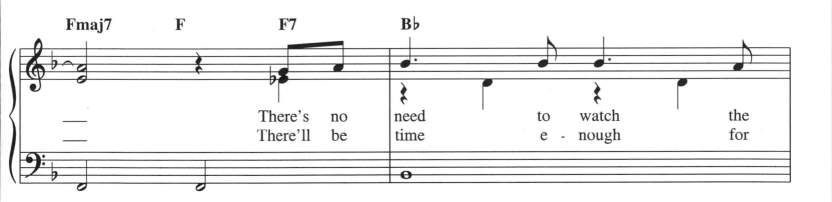

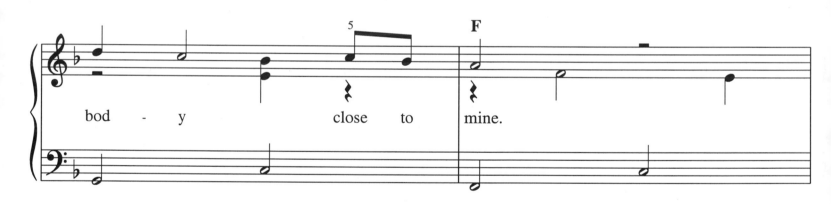

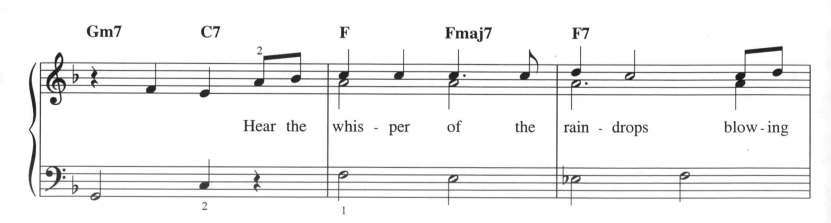

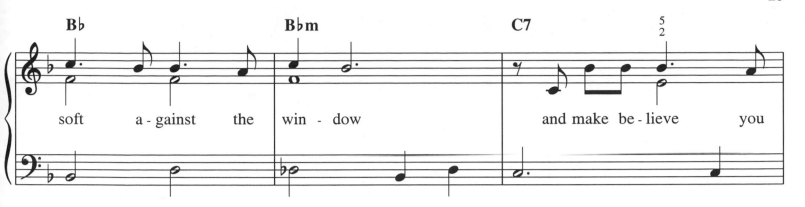

soft a - gainst the win - dow and make be - lieve you

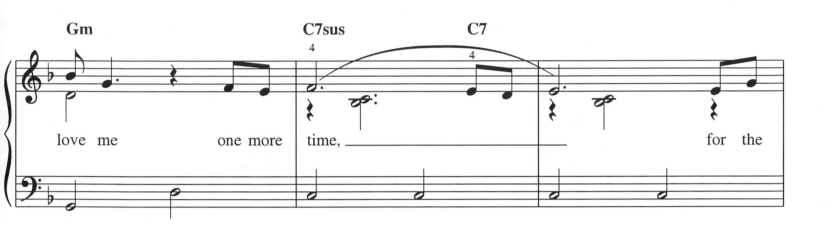

love me one more time, ____ for the

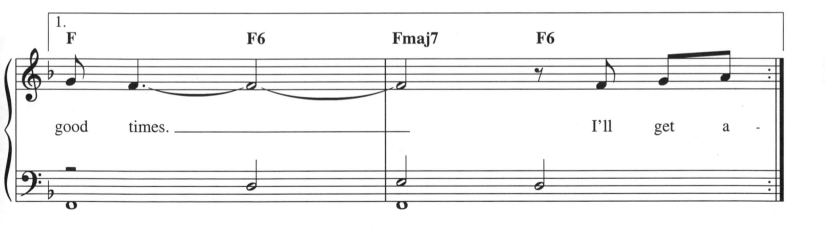

good times. ____ I'll get a -

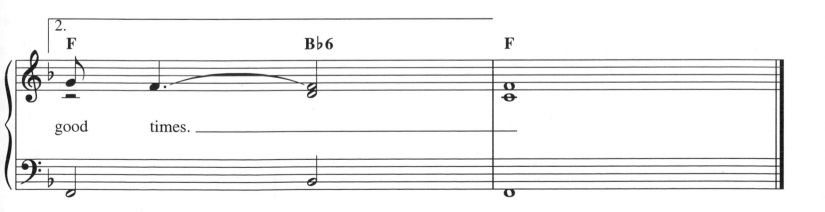

good times. ____

FRIENDS IN LOW PLACES

Words and Music by DEWAYNE BLACKWELL
and EARL BUD LEE

Moderately, with a beat

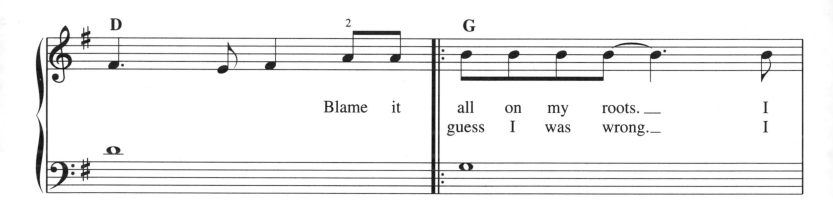

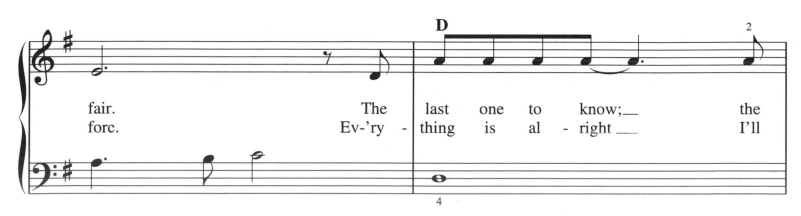

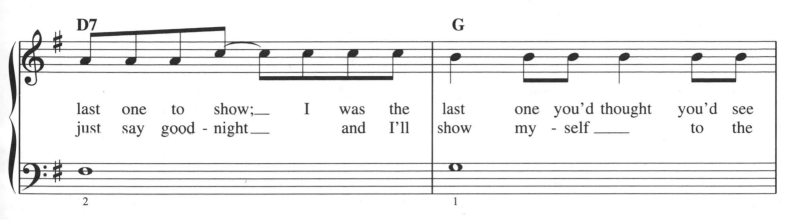

last one to show;___ I was the last one you'd thought you'd see
just say good - night___ and I'll show my - self ____ to the

there. _____ And I saw the sur - prise ___ and the
door. _____ Hey, I did - n't mean _ to

fear in his eyes___ when I took his glass of cham -
cause a big scene.___ Just give me an ho - ur and

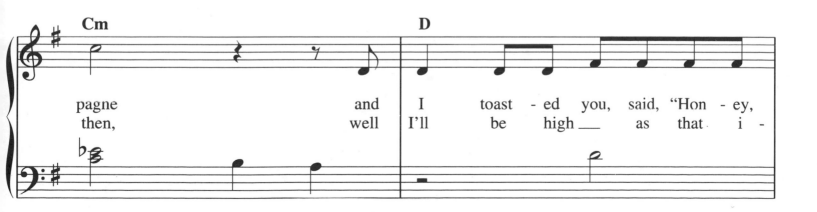

pagne and I toast - ed you, said, "Hon - ey,
then, well I'll be high ___ as that i -

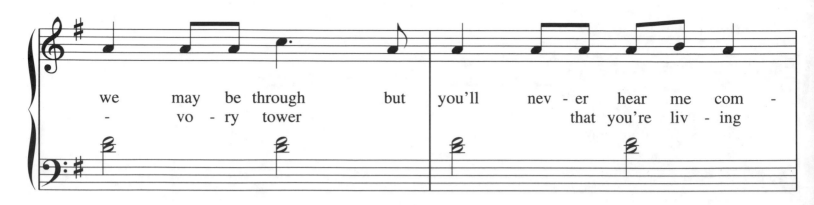

we may be through but you'll nev - er hear me com -
- vo - ry tower that you're liv - ing

plain." 'Cause I've got friends in
in.

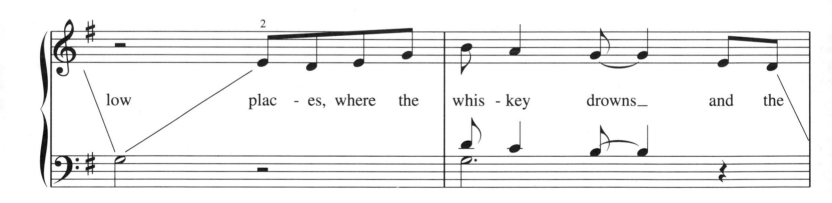

low plac - es, where the whis - key drowns and the

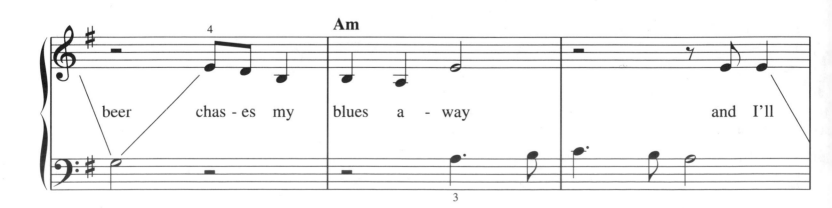

beer chas - es my blues a - way and I'll

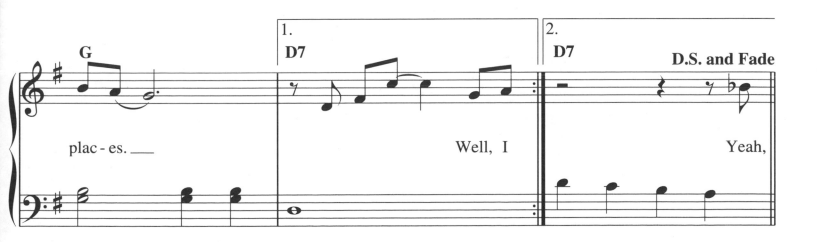

THE GAMBLER

Words and Music by
DON SCHLITZ

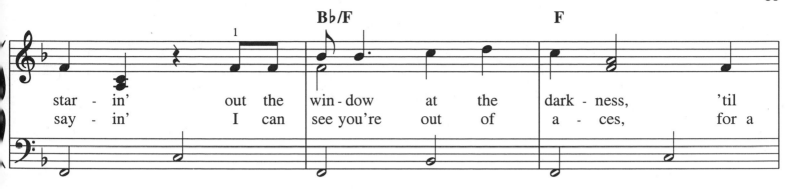

star - in'   out the   win - dow   at the   dark - ness,   'til
say - in'   I can see you're   out of   a - ces,   for a

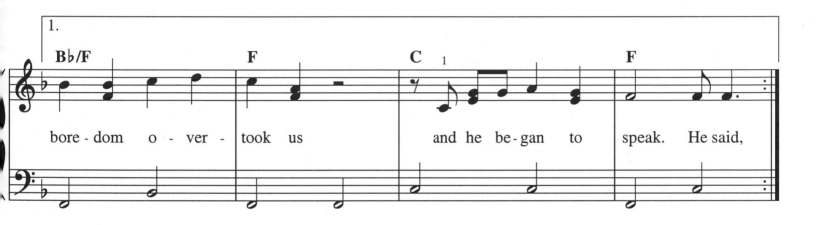

1.

bore - dom o - ver - took us   and he be - gan to   speak.   He said,

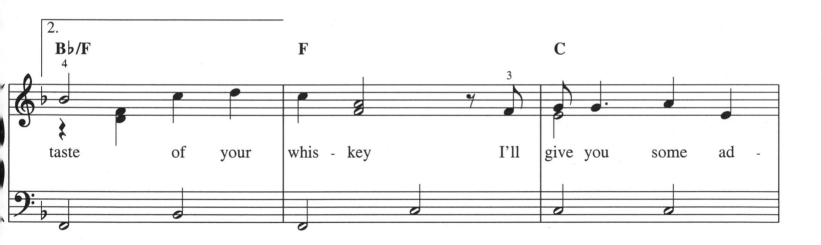

2.

taste   of your   whis - key   I'll   give you   some   ad -

vice.   So I   hand - ed   him my

36

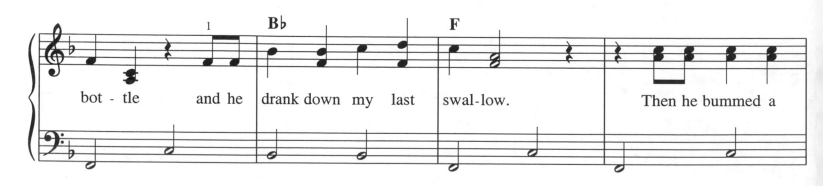

bot - tle   and he   drank down my last   swal-low.   Then he bummed a

cig - a - rette __   and asked me   for   a   light.   And the

night got death-ly   qui - et,   and his face lost all ex -

pres - sion   said, "If you're gon - na play __ the   game boy   you got-ta

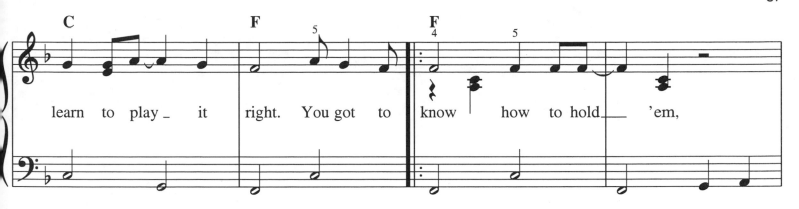

learn to play __ it right. You got to

know how to hold __ 'em, know when to fold __ 'em,

know when to

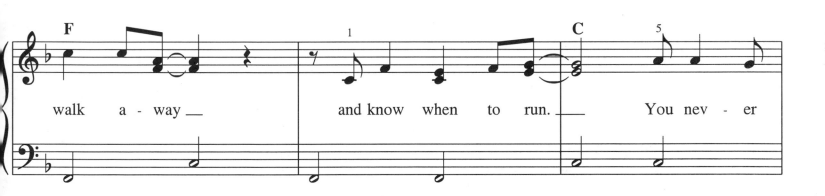

walk a - way __ and know when to run. __ You nev - er

count your mon - ey when you're sit - tin' at the ta -

- ble. There'll be time e - nough _ for count - in' when the deal - in's

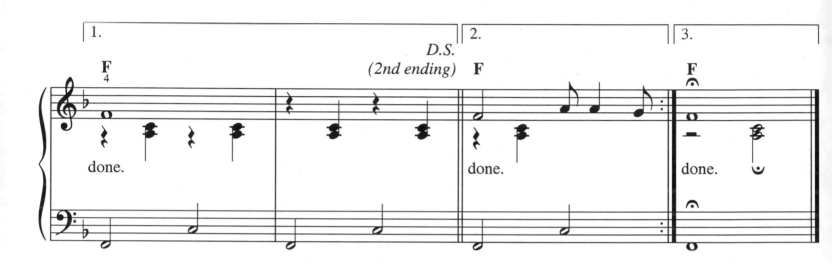

done. done. done.

Additional Lyrics

Ev'ry gambler knows that the secret to survivin'
Is knowin' what to throw away and knowin' what to keep.
'Cause ev'ry hand's a winner and ev'ry hand's a loser
And the best that you can hope for is to die in your sleep.

And when he'd finished speakin', he turned back towards the window
Crushed out his cigarette and faded off to sleep.
And somewhere in the darkness the gambler he broke even
But in his final words I found an ace that I could keep. You've got to...*(Chorus)*

HE STOPPED LOVING HER TODAY

Words and Music by BOBBY BRADDOCK
and CURLY PUTMAN

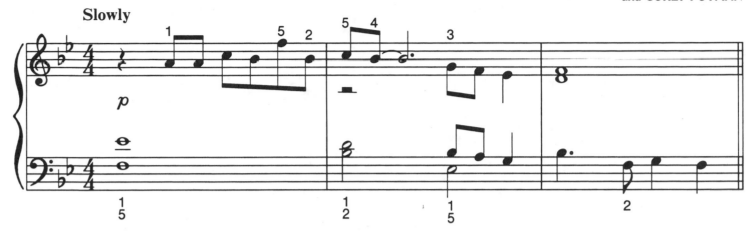

1. He said, "I'll love you 'til I die."
2. He kept some let-ters by his bed
3. *Instrumental*

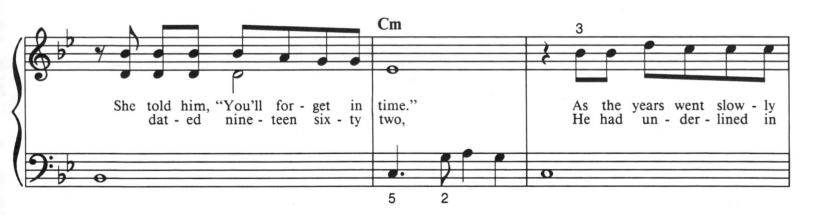

She told him, "You'll for-get in time."
dat-ed nine-teen six-ty two,

As the years went slow-ly
He had un-der-lined in

by
red

she still preyed up-on his mind.
ev'-ry sin-gle "I love you."

He kept her pic - ture on his wall,
Spoken: You know she came to see him one last time,

went half cra - zy now and then,
but I did - n't see no tears,
we all won - dered if she would.

But he still loved her through it all,
All dressed up to go a - way,
And it came run - ning through my mind,

hop - ing she'd come back a - gain. _____
first time I'd seen him smile in years. _____
"This time he's over her for good." _____

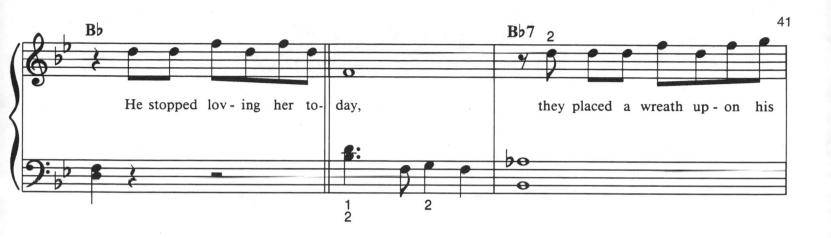

He stopped lov-ing her to- day, they placed a wreath up-on his

door,___ And soon they'll car-ry him a - way;___

He stopped lov-ing her to- day.___

He stopped lov-ing her to- day.___

GRANDPA
(Tell Me 'Bout the Good Old Days)

Words and Music by
JAMIE O'HARA

Grand - pa, ___ tell me 'bout the good old days. ___
Grand - pa, ___ ev - 'ry - thing is chang-in' fast. ___

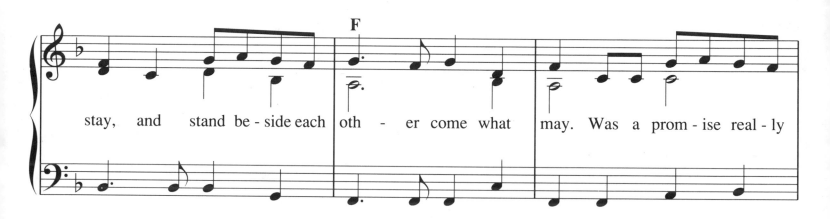

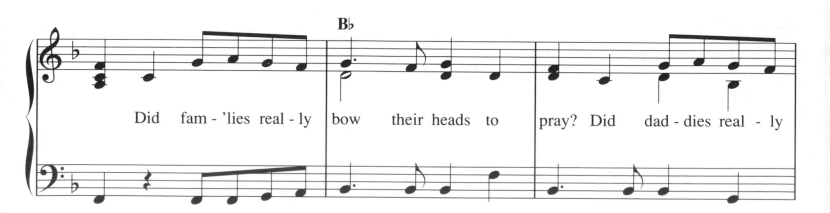

HEARTACHES BY THE NUMBER

Words and Music by
HARLAN HOWARD

Moderately bright, in 2 (𝅗𝅥 = 1 beat)

Heart - ache Num - ber One was when you
Heart - ache Num - ber Three was when you

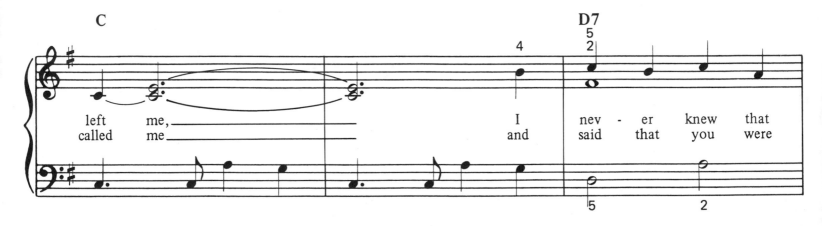

left me, _____ I
called me _____ and

nev - er knew that
said that knew you were

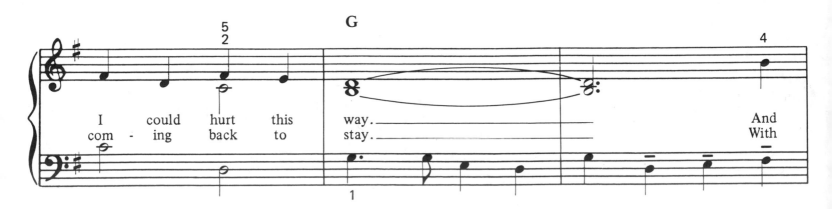

I could hurt this way. _____ And
com - ing back to stay. _____ With

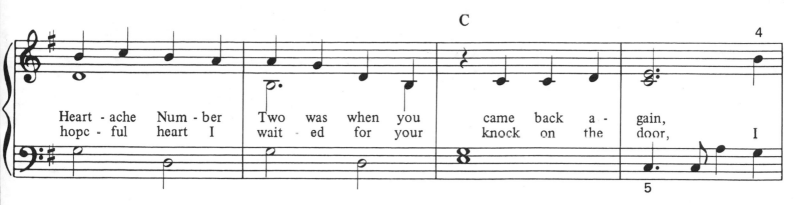

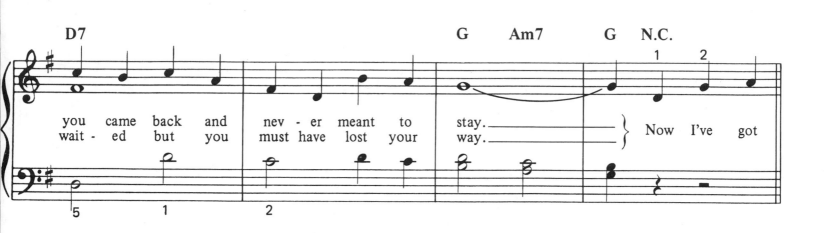

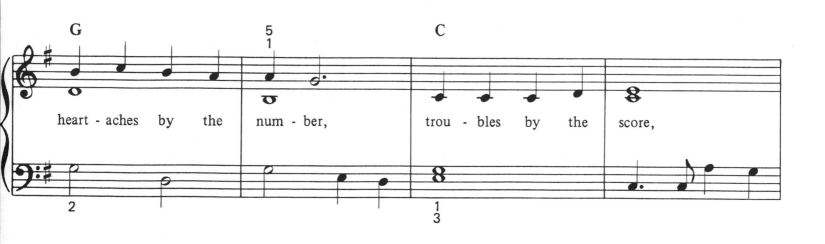

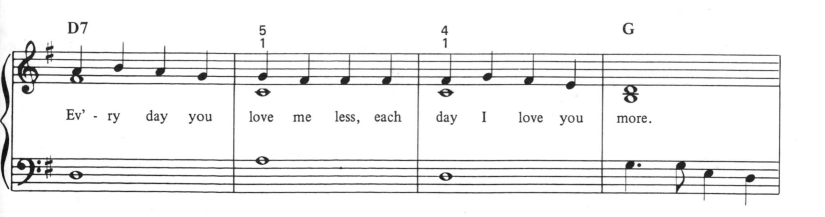

48

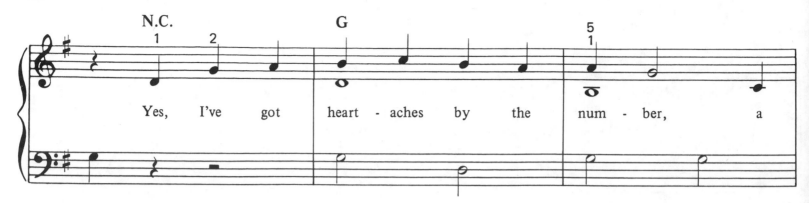

Yes, I've got heart - aches by the num - ber, a

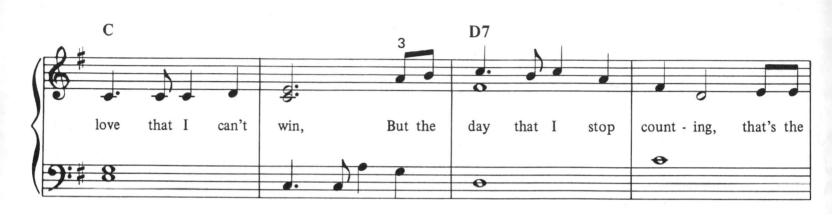

love that I can't win, But the day that I stop count - ing, that's the

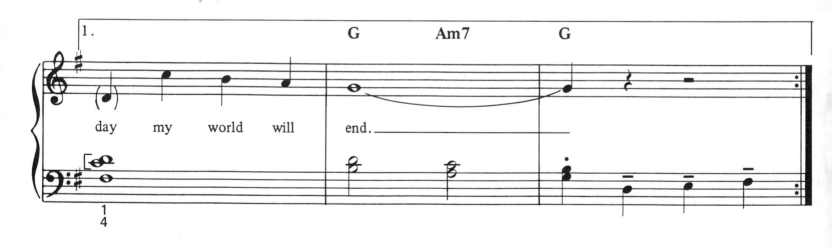

day my world will end.

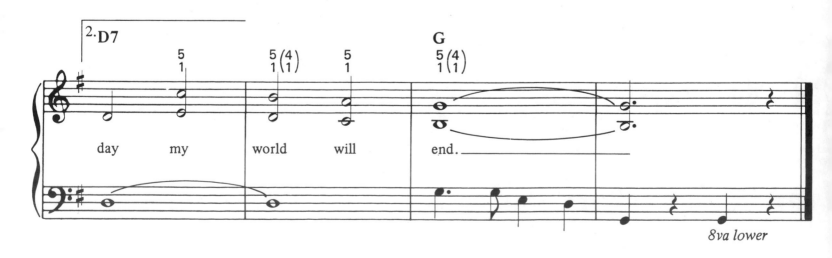

day my world will end.

8va lower

HERE'S A QUARTER
(Call Someone Who Cares)

Words and Music by
TRAVIS TRITT

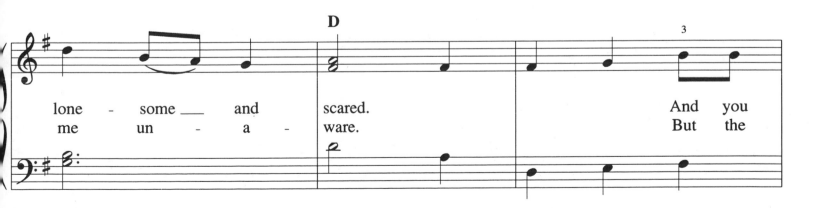

50

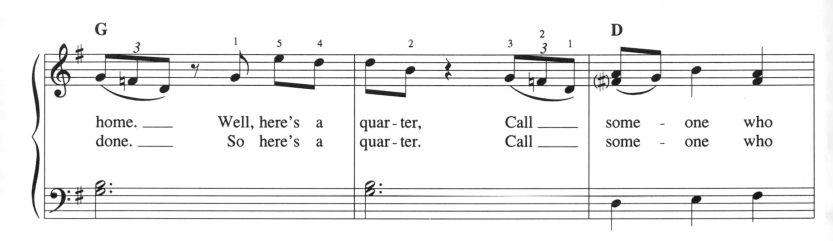

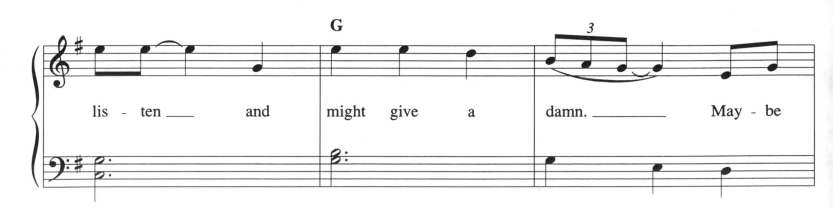

D.S. al Coda

Girl, I _____

CODA

cares.

Yeah, here's a

quar - ter. ___ Call ___ some - one ___ who cares. _____

_____ Yeah, _____ yeah. _____

rit.

KING OF THE ROAD

Words and Music by
ROGER MILLER

Moderate Swing (♪♪ is played ♪♪)

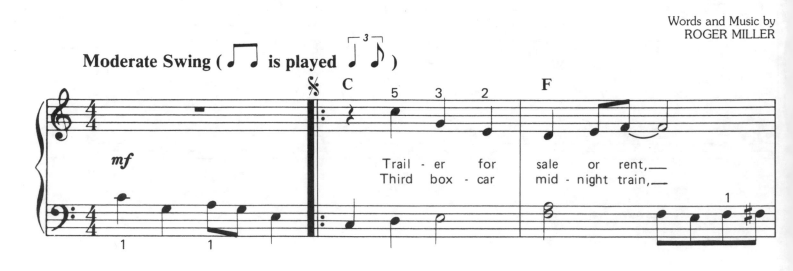

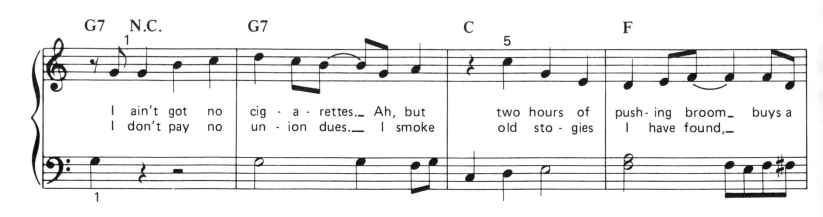

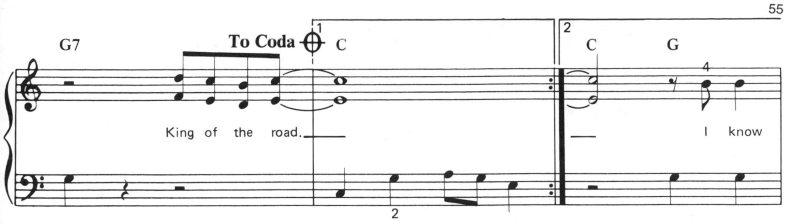

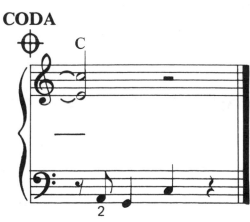

MAKE THE WORLD GO AWAY

Words and Music by
HANK COCHRAN

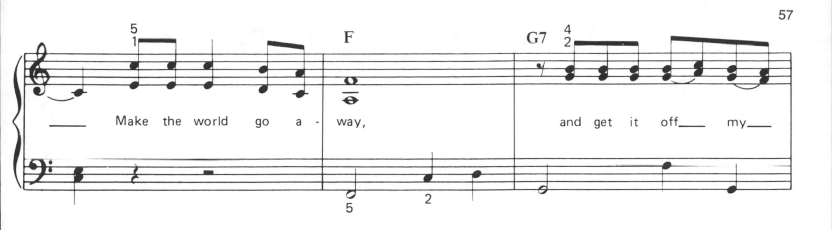

Make the world go a- way, and get it off___ my___

shoul - ders, say the things you used to say,

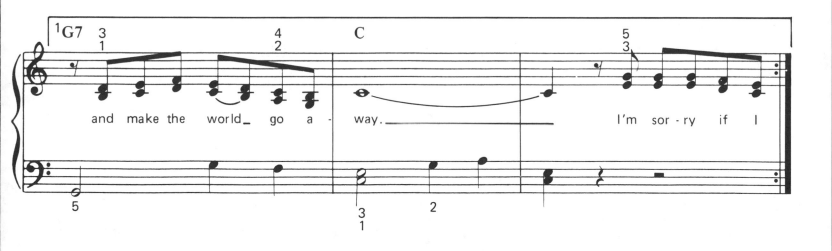

and make the world_ go a - way.____ I'm sor-ry if I

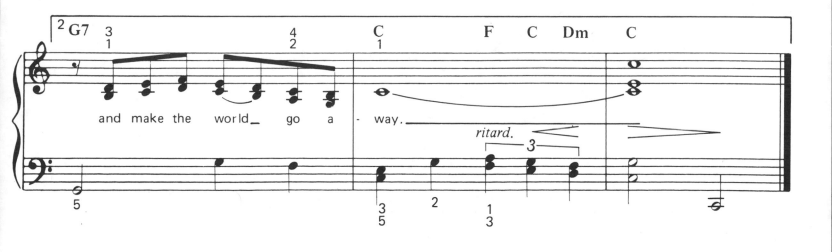

and make the world_ go a - way.____ ritard.

OH, LONESOME ME

Words and Music by
DON GIBSON

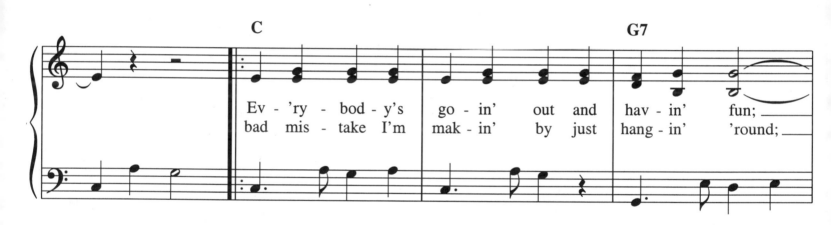

Ev - 'ry - bod - y's | go - in' out and | hav - in' fun; ____
bad mis - take I'm | mak - in' by just | hang - in' 'round; ____

I'm | just a fool for | stay - in' home and | hav - in' none. ____
I | know that I should | have some fun and | paint the town. ____

boys with all her charms, _____ but I still love her

so, and broth - er don't you know I'd wel - come her right

back here in my arms. __ Well, there must be some way

I can lose these lone-some blues, _____ for - get a - bout the

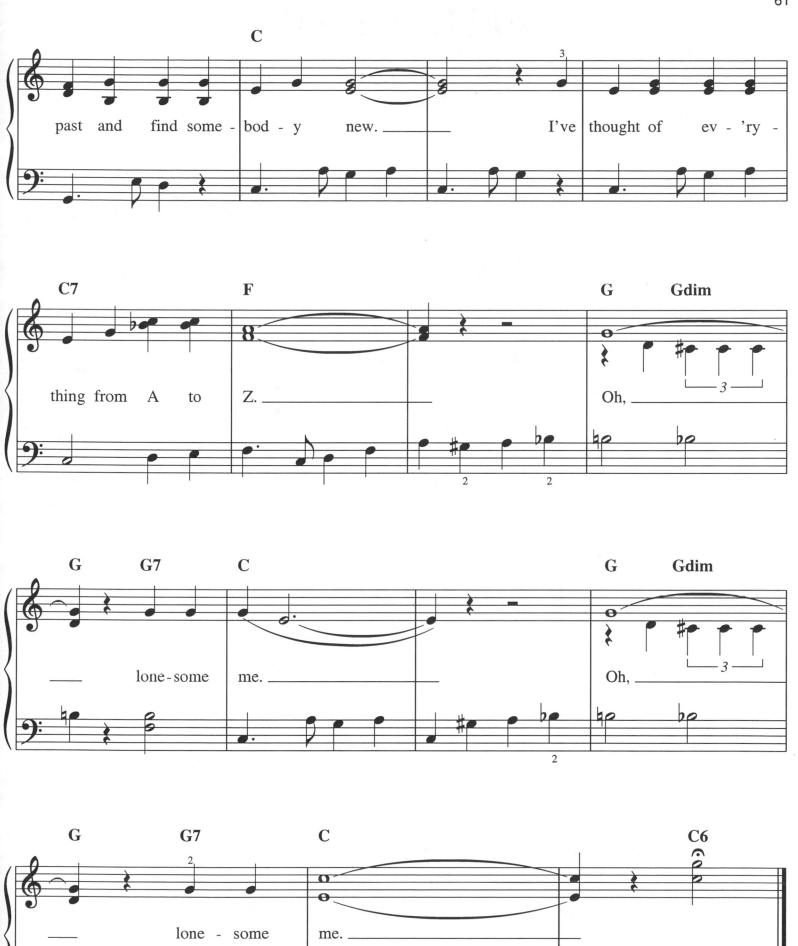

RELEASE ME

Words and Music by ROBERT YOUNT,
EDDIE MILLER and DUB WILLIAMS

Moderately slow

TENNESSEE WALTZ

Words and Music by REDD STEWART
and PEE WEE KING

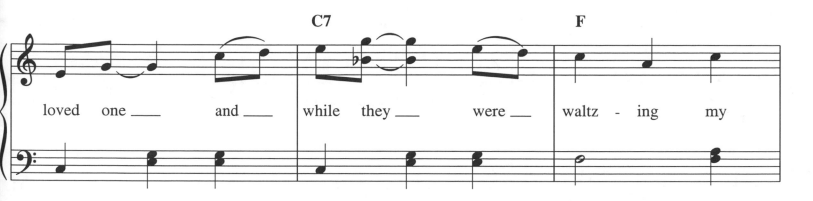

loved one ___ and ___ while they ___ were ___ waltz - ing my

friend stole my sweet - heart from me. _____

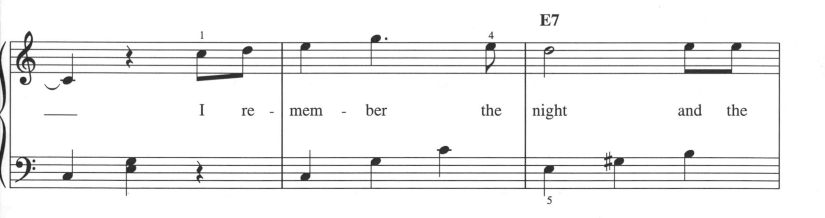

___ I re - mem - ber the night and the

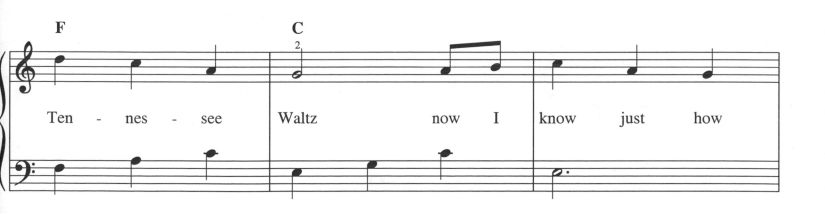

Ten - nes - see Waltz now I know just how

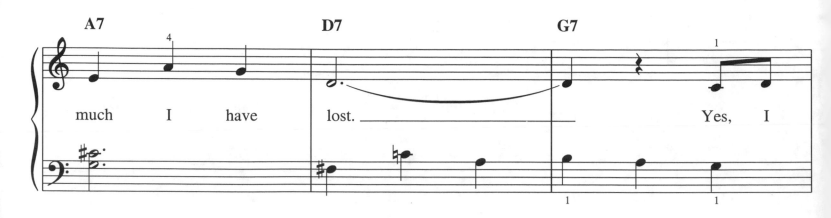

much I have lost. _____ Yes, I

lost my ___ lit - tle dar - lin' ___ the ___ night they ___ were ___

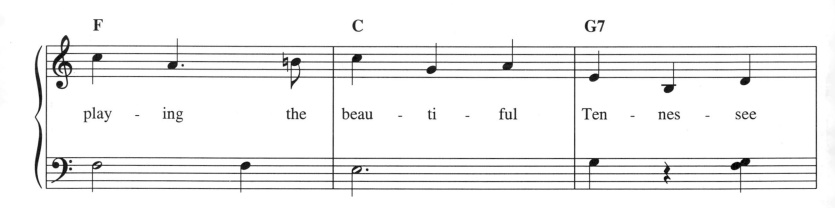

play - ing the beau - ti - ful Ten - nes - see

1.
Waltz. _____ I was

2.
Waltz. *rit.*

WALKIN' AFTER MIDNIGHT

Lyrics by DON HECHT
Music by ALAN W. BLOCK

68

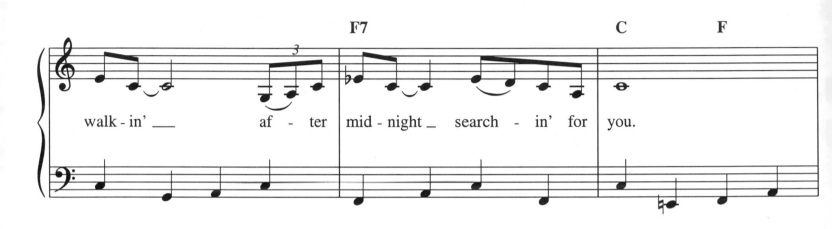

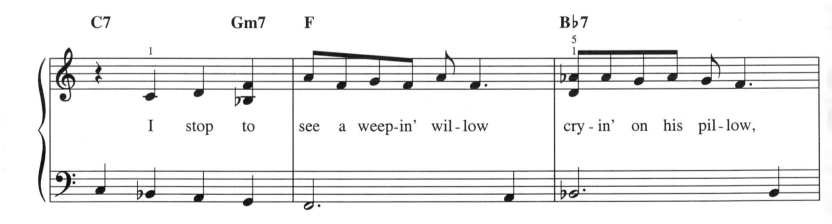

WHEN WILL I BE LOVED

Words and Music by
PHIL EVERLY

YOU DON'T KNOW ME

Words and Music by CINDY WALKER
and EDDY ARNOLD

know me.
For I nev-er knew the

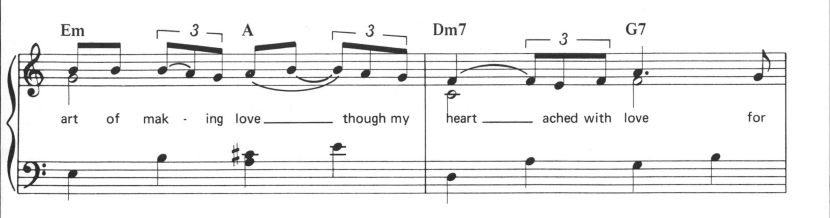

art of mak-ing love _____ though my heart _____ ached with love for

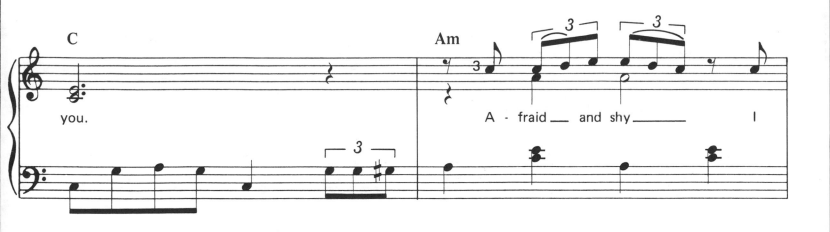

you.
A - fraid __ and shy _____ I

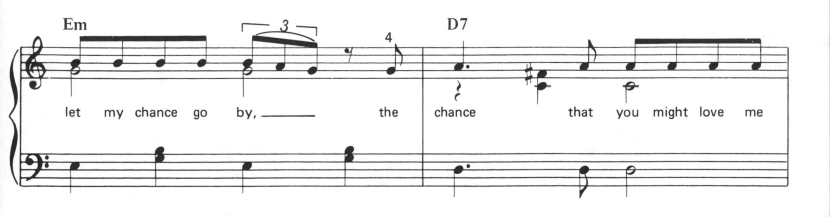

let my chance go by, _____ the chance that you might love me

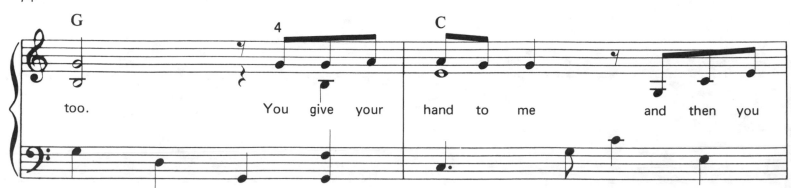

too. You give your hand to me and then you

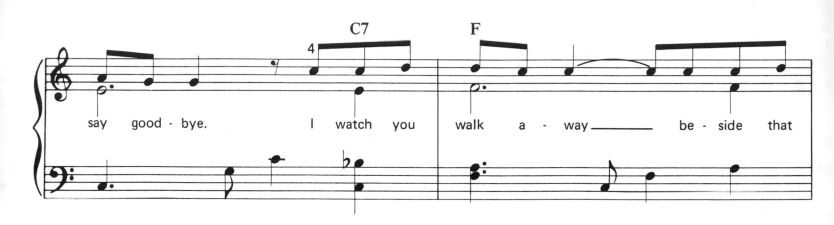

say good-bye. I watch you walk a-way_____ be-side that

luck-y guy. You'll nev-er nev-er know_____ the one who

loves you so; no, you don't know me.

YOU NEEDED ME

Words and Music by
RANDY GOODRUM

I cried a tear, you wiped it dry.
hand when it was cold.
I was con-
When I was

fused, you cleared my mind. I sold my soul. you bought it
lost you took me home. You gave me hope, When I was

back for me and held me up and gave me dig - ni - ty. Some - how you
at the end, and turned my lies back in - to truth a - gain. You e - ven

76

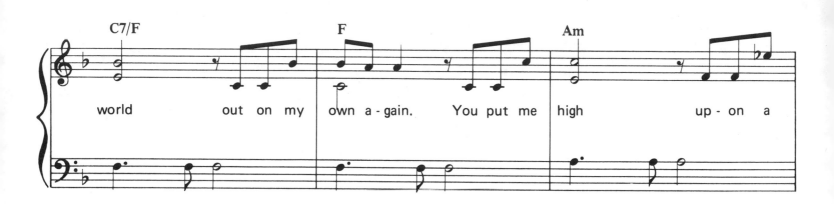

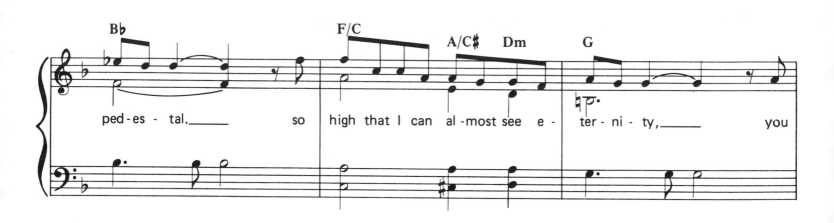

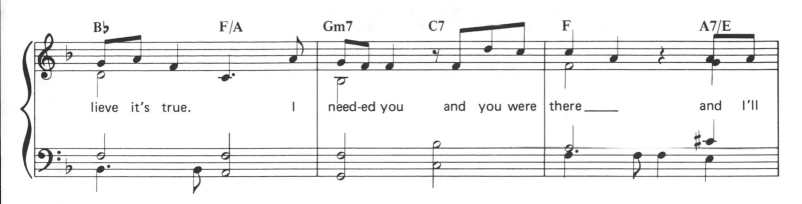

YOUR CHEATIN' HEART

Words and Music by
HANK WILLIAMS

Moderately

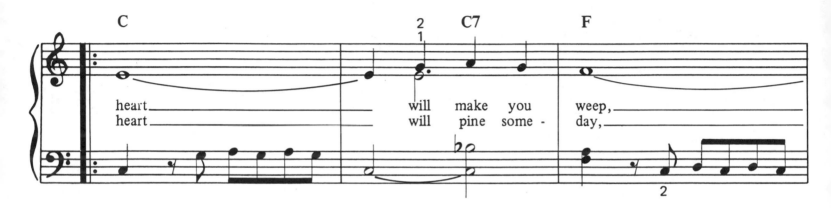

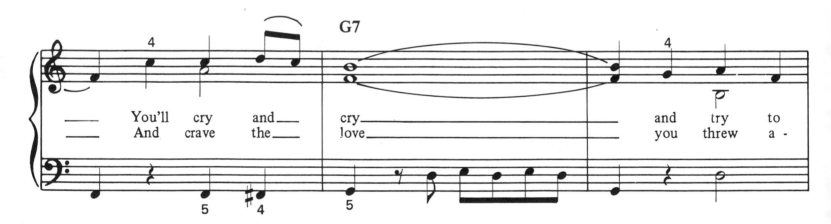

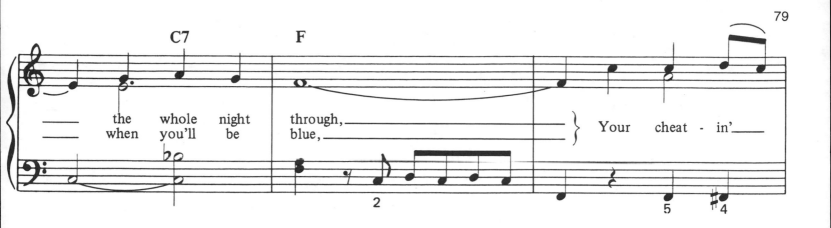

the whole night through,
when you'll be blue,
Your cheat - in'

heart will tell on you.

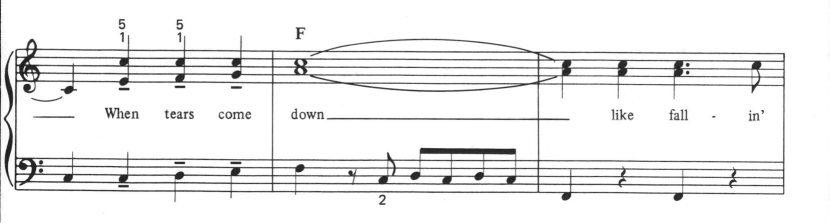

When tears come down like fall - in'

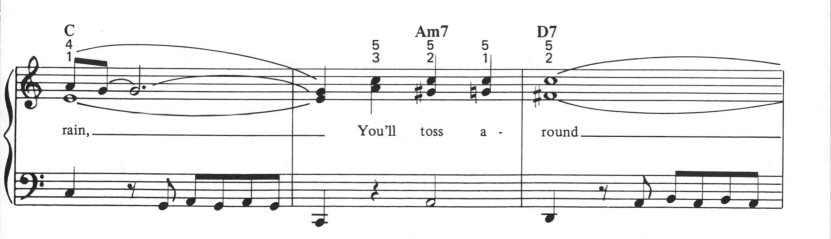

rain, You'll toss a - round

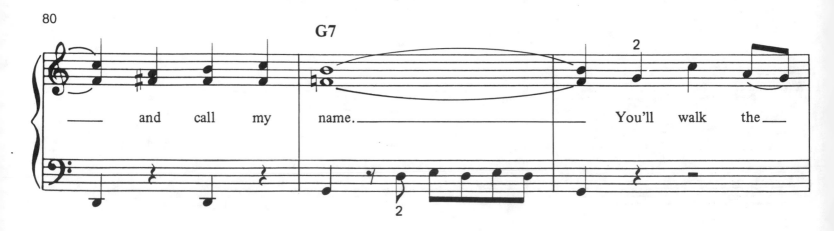

and call my name._____ You'll walk the___

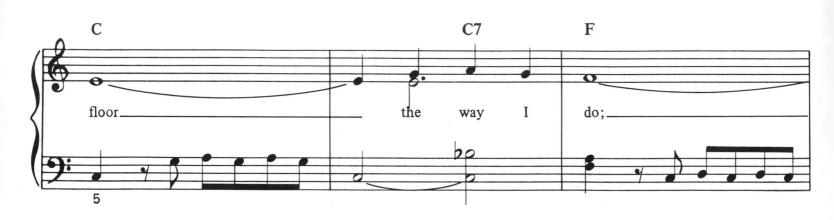

floor_____ the way I do;_____

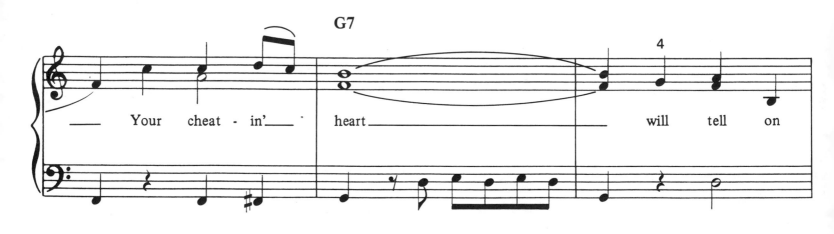

___ Your cheat - in'___ heart_____ will tell on

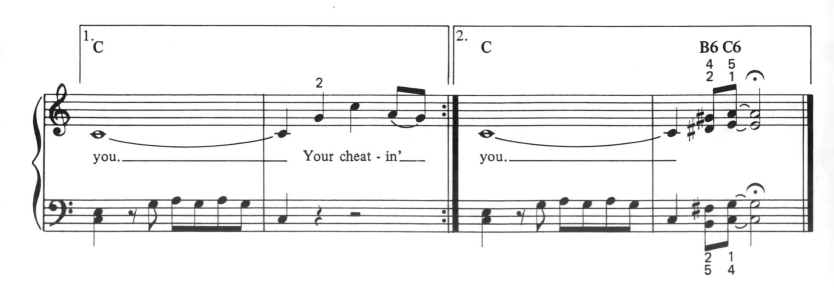

you._____ Your cheat - in'___ you._____